The second book in the
Chimo Heritage Series.

October Stranger

George Kenny

in collaboration with Denis Lacroix

 chimo

Designed and produced at Dreadnaught
24 Sussex Avenue
Toronto Canada

ISBN 0 920344 04 6

INTRODUCTION

Early in 1977, the Association
for Native Development in the
Performing and Visual Arts was
invited to be Canada's represen-
tative at the Sixth International
Theatre Festival in Monaco,
September 1st 1977. It was more
than just an invitation – it was a
challenge. This would be the first
time that Canada was represented
at an International Theatre
Festival by a Native production.

On accepting the invitation, I
was determined that our production would be a play that was
written, produced, directed, and
performed by Native people. I
realized, after some searching, that
there were very few appropriate
plays written by Native people that
related to contemporary situations.
Having become acquainted with
Mr George Kenny in his efforts to

v

prepare some of his poems and short stories for publication, and recognizing his particular talent for writing dialogue, I suggested that he try his hand at writing for theatre. After several discussions, he agreed to the suggestion and decided to prepare a script based on his poem, 'October Stranger'. This poem describes the kind of conflicts that many young Native people are facing at the present time.

We were also fortunate in procuring the services, (as the director for the production) of Mr Denis Lacroix, who was willing to share his theatrical experience with George Kenny by collaborating in the writing of the play.

I must say that this undertaking was not a simple one. It involved long hours of examining the characters and situations described in George Kenny's book, *Indians Don't Cry*. It must also be acknowledged that the cast played an important role in developing the script.

The final reward was received from the audiences that responded enthusiastically to the performances, both in Canada and in Monaco. Notable were the comments on the play's humour, tenderness, and poignancy. As one observer in Monaco indicated, it is a play that provides a better understanding of Native people in Canada, and a script that would be welcomed by any theatre group in the world.

The Association is pleased to have initiated this major step in the progress of Native theatre in Canada and trusts that it will serve as an example to other Native writers and performers.

James H. Buller

Executive-Director
Association for Native
Development in the Performing &
Visual Arts.

For the migrating Native people; for Jim Buller, Denis Lacroix, the cast and all those who assisted in the production of *October Stranger*.

The premier performance of *October Stranger* was at Todmorden Mills Theatre in Toronto on the twenty-ninth of July, nineteen-seventy-eight.

CAST

JOHN Sherman Maness
IDA Shirley Cheechoo
JOSH Adrian Winter
LIZ Marianne Jones
PAUL James Whetung

DIRECTOR Denis Lacroix
EXECUTIVE PRODUCER James Buller
PRODUCTION MANAGER Diane Mitchell
STAGE MANAGER Donna Noonan

*Time: The Present. Morning in
mid-September. The time of
year is when nature begins its
preparation for autumn and
winter to come. For the
characters in the play, it is the
time when they too are faced
with the possibility of change. In
the distance the fading sound of
an outboard motor is heard.
Though it is a clear day, mist
hangs over the lake surface like
white sheets.*
*Place: On an Ojibway Indian
reservation. By a lakeshore. At
the edge of the beach, in centre
stage, a dock projects toward the
audience.*
*Reality: John the author as his
daily self.*

*Scene: As the play opens, John —
in sports jacket, shirt with tie,
dress slacks — comes on stage.
He carries a brief-case.
He walks about the stage,
pauses periodically, reflecting
various moods.
John notices a manuscript lying
on the dock. He smiles as he
flips through it. Then he exits.*

TRANSITION INTO INTROSPECT

*Next: The four other characters
come on stage, sounding out a
fading outboard motor. They
line up, two on each side of the
dock.*

*John re-enters, he is in a rush,
frantically waving an old
fishing cap.*

JOHN Hey Dad, your cap! Hold the
boat! Hey, you forgot your cap!
Oh damn!
*John seats himself on the dock
pondering. He hears something.
The Chorus comes up behind
him.*
Who is it?

CHORUS Guess!

JOHN Gee...I don't know. Beautiful
morning.

JOSH *looking on audience* It is, isn't
it?

JOHN Yeah, sure is.

IDA *steps up close to John* What are
you doing with your father's
cap?

3

JOHN I guess he forgot it. I tried to catch him…

CHORUS We saw you.

PAUL *bends down to one side of John* You must be getting out of shape, not like your father.

JOHN For a 64-year-old man, he sure is in great shape.

LIZ He sure is.
Steps beside Paul. Puts hand on John's shoulder.
He woke you up and cooked breakfast for you.

JOHN That's my dad, a great cook and the best fish guide in all of Ontario.

JOSH *also leans to talk to John* Where's he going?

JOHN Silver Lake Lodge. The tourist lodge built for Americans. It's about twenty miles from here.

4

CHORUS We know.

IDA *crouches beside John* How long
will he be away this time?

JOHN About a week.

LIZ That means he won't be back in
time to see you off. If you do
leave on this morning's plane.
*Comes behind Paul so as to
stand behind John.*

JOHN I suppose.

CHORUS *stands* Do you have to leave?
*Pulls back. A couple of seconds
pose of Chorus.*

JOHN I still ask myself that every
day.
*Chorus turns and walks off.
Only Ida stays*

TRANSITION TO REALITY

IDA You know you could stay and

get that new Band
Administrator's job.

*Beside John on dock. Kneels,
hand on shoulder.*

JOHN I want to be a writer, not some
clerk behind a desk.

IDA Being a Band Administrator
isn't so bad John. With your
good education you could really
help our people to a better life.
You always said you wanted to
help.

JOHN I know I did.

IDA Do you know what my mother
said when your father asked if
you could marry me?

JOHN Suppose I did stay and we got
married. Would that make you
happy?

IDA Why not? Remember all the

happy summers we've spent together?

JOHN Suppose I wasn't satisfied and I wanted to leave. Would you come with me?

IDA Who would look after my mother? She has only me.

JOHN We could take her with us.

IDA And your father?

JOHN We'd take him too.

IDA To a town? Or a city like Toronto? You know how far it is to the city.

JOHN Yeah.

IDA *standing* And you know how different the city is from our home here in Lac Seul. *Takes hand off John's shoulder.* I've been to the city too. Our parents are used to this way of

life. They are used to the
natural light of the sun by day
and the moon at night. A city is
so big and no one knows one
another. They could never get
used to that now.

JOHN I know.

IDA In the city, they would end up
living the rest of their lives like
the white people there – like my
old Uncle Daniel in Winnipeg. I
remember when I saw him in a
Senior Citizens' high-rise
apartment building. He talked
in Ojibway about the wigwams
and how he could remember the
children's laughter. I remember
promising him, 'We'll make
room in our house later. Then
you can come home to Lac Seul
again.' But, the next time I
heard about him was when I

8

read a letter to my mother asking her to make funeral arrangements...Poor old Uncle Daniel – we are taught to take care of our elders. John – it's our way of life.

JOHN You're right. They couldn't come with us.

IDA This past winter, I used to go visit your mother. It was before your mother got very sick. One evening, as I went to visit, it was real cold outside and it was so nice and warm when I went in. Your mother – she was alone.

JOHN And Mom, she got up, poked at the fire, and made a fresh pot of tea...

IDA And while we were talking, your father came home...

JOHN I can see him now.

9

*Gets up and starts to
pantomime his father.*
He comes in, brushes the snow
off his moccasins, then he
unbuttons his Hudson Bay
parka and just grinning away,
he tells my mom what he got –
'I got ten beavers, four mink,
and five rabbits, Elsie' – and
Mom was just smiling…

IDA *gets up beside John and
pantomimes taking off coat* She
got up and helped your father
take off his parka and she said,
'You're a good trapper, my
husband.
Embraces John.
I'm happy to be your woman.'

JOHN And Dad said, 'I'm happy to be
your man.'

IDA *looking at John* We could be like that.

JOHN I'm not sure it would work. Me, as a trapper? No way. The last time I went trapping with my Dad this past Christmas, I found that what I've learned during my years off the Reserve has separated me from his – my life style, the way I feel. It's different from his.

IDA You could learn your father's ways.

JOHN I don't think so. Hah!
Steps up.
The time I went with my Dad, he asked me to stay on the shore of a beaver pond. He gave me his .22 rifle to shoot a beaver when it would come out

of the hole. I didn't like the idea
of shooting a beaver...but my
dad asked me to...I had my
camera, and really, that's what
I wanted to do, get a
photograph of a beaver when it
came out of that hole in the ice.
Turns front.
All of a sudden, there it was,
right in front of me.

IDA *stepping up to John* What did
you do...?

JOHN I guess, obeying my father was
more important because I
dropped my camera, grabbed
the rifle and shot it.
*Almost mimes shooting the
beaver.*

IDA See, you could learn....

JOHN And as I watched it dying, I

realized – No, I don't want to kill any animal for a living. I know it's necessary for my father – he's a trapper, hunter, fisherman. But me, I want to be a writer – No Ida, my father and I, we live in two different worlds.

Ida turns to top of dock. Sits facing back.

I wish it wasn't that way, but it is....

TRANSITION TO INTROSPECT

Moves off dock Stage Right. Josh enters, sneaks to Front Left and does loon call. A loon's call is heard in the distance.

What a beautiful loon call...

That's a sound I'll miss when
I leave.

*Josh freezes before he reaches
lake. Ida turns to Josh then
freezes for the rest of this scene.*

That sound wasn't a real loon.
It was Josh. He sure fooled me.
I remember asking him, 'Hey
Josh, how long have you been
making those sounds?'

TRANSITION TO REALITY

*Josh comes alive. Moves toward
John.*

JOSH Ever since I started
painting...a few years ago.

JOHN You call birds for your
paintings?

JOSH Not only birds, but animals too.

October Stranger

John and Josh move to Stage Left.

JOHN *indicating pail* What are you doing here so early?

JOSH I need to get some water for a painting I'm doing.

JOHN You must be planning to use one helluva large canvas.

JOSH You bet. I'm going to paint the largest goddamn tree you ever saw.

Puts pail down.

A white pine, four thousand feet tall.

JOHN White pines don't grow that high!

JOSH They do in my mind; when people look at my painting, they're going to think so too. That white pine tree will reach

high into the sky and around
its boughs there'll be clouds and
some seagulls flying around the
height of it.

JOHN What?

JOSH The kind that fly to eat over the
liquid movement of rivers.

JOHN That sounds like my poetry.

JOSH Seagull eats to fly from liquid
motions of lakes...

*Begins to move playfully around
Centre Stage. John joins him
while they quote lines.*

JOHN Stones his eyes, roving for
scaly morsels...

JOSH Fillet-knifed his beak, slashing
for finned portions...

JOHN Portions for power in his white
wings...

JOSH Morsels for strength in his
flight tendons...

JOHN Seagull flies to eat power portions...

JOSH Seagull eats to fly strong morsels...

JOHN Over motioning rivers...

JOSH Over moving lakes...

BOTH For the circle reasons of his seagull seasons...

They stop Centre Stage.

JOHN You should be a poet too. Not only a painter.

JOSH You like to paint with words on paper – me, I like to paint with acrylics on canvas to get my meanings of life across. When we were in high school, you always got a kick out of my paintings.

Goes to the shoreline to get some water.

JOHN I liked that one you did of the

moose, the painting that blew everyone's mind. I remember asking you, 'Hey Josh, what the hell does that painting mean?' *Josh rinses his pail and throws some water towards John.*

JOSH Be damned if I know. *Josh freezes.*

INTROSPECT

JOHN *to audience – three feet Stage Left of dock* I like the painting of the moose, the king of the northern forest! I wrote a poem about that painting with its colors in shades of scarlet and blackest of black lines for the massive antlers of the moose. *Pauses. Turns to Josh who is on*

stepping stones on the shoreline
and filling up his pail.

TRANSITION TO REALITY

You really like my poetry?
Josh moves toward John.
JOSH Yeah, but I like my paintings
better.
Freezes at end of his line.

TRANSITION TO INTROSPECT

JOHN *walking Stage Left, turning to*
audience As far as I was
concerned, no one could paint
like Josh.
IDA *getting up, walking up to John*
and then off You could help our
people if you stay.

Josh walks off with Ida Stage Left. Liz enters Stage Right.

JOHN I always felt that I wanted to help our Reserve develop and Chief Samuel asked me if I wanted the new Band Administrator job.

LIZ So, you're thinking of staying now?

JOHN Sure, why not? It might be a good job.

LIZ And you think being Band Administrator is going to be enough of a challenge for you?

JOHN I didn't say that!

LIZ What about your dreams of being a professional writer? You can't become one out here.
Paul enters.

JOHN Professional?

LIZ Yes, professional.

PAUL Sure, we can all go to the city to become professionals. You a writer, her an entertainer, and me, a dancer!
Sound of Plane by Chorus members backstage.
There! Just over the trees! That can't be our airplane yet. It's too early. It's headed north carrying supplies.
Turning to John
That doesn't give you much time to make up your mind.
Looks, steps off riser to John and exits Stage Left.

TRANSITION TO REALITY

LIZ *stepping down* What's the matter, John?
JOHN It seems that everyone knows

what I should do with my life.
Sometimes I just want to run
away.
*Goes from Centre Stage to Stage
Right.*

LIZ *sitting on Large Riser* You
were good at that too.
John turns to Liz.
I remember the year we got
shipped down to Sault Ste.
Marie and you ran away in
October.

JOHN *sitting next to Liz* God, I
wanted to get home. I hopped a
freight train and rode a day and
a half to get to Sioux Lookout.

LIZ And when the principal of the
residential school asked
everyone in the dining room if
they'd seen you ... I was so
scared I started to cry. *pause*

Why did you come back?

JOHN Because my mother felt I
should finish my education.

LIZ *turning straight forward* I
liked your mother, Johnny. She
was beautiful.

JOHN *nodding* My father always said
he was the luckiest Indian on
the whole Reserve.

LIZ *turning to John* Even as she
grew older, she seemed to grow
more beautiful.

JOHN *nodding* Even as lines formed
around her eyes, lines like the
weaving of medicine spiders,
she would still keep her chin
uplifted, her black eyes flashing
with pride and happiness...It
was her spirit that made her
what she was...

LIZ *looking at John* Do you think

Ida has that same spirit?
Looks away.
Or will she grow fat from
eating potatoes and bannock?

JOHN *getting up and turning to Liz* It
doesn't matter.

LIZ *getting up and going to Stage
Left* It does matter. I know
what you're like. Times I was
with you on the streets in
Toronto or even on the train to
get there. I saw you looking at
all those white women in their
short skirts and pantyhose.
And hey, remember that time
we were walking by the Silver
Dollar in Toronto last spring? I
had stopped just a little behind
you to look at a sign and the
next thing I know there you

were talking to some blonde
hooker.
Steps on dock.

JOHN *coming on to dock and looking
almost Front* Well, I didn't
know she was a prostitute.

LIZ *grabbing John's arm, pulls him
around and steps up to him* Got
a match, big boy?
Waits for John's reaction to joke.
Yeah, I heard her, and you were
so eager to please, fumbling
around for your lighter and
then she said, 'Lonesome, big
buck? If you are, I can fix that.
I'm good...'
Bumps John off dock.
And she had on one of those low
V-necked sweaters and you
looked right down.

Follows John off dock and gives him a playful shove.

JOHN *looking a bit puzzled* No, I didn't look down...

LIZ Sure you did!

JOHN What is this anyway?

LIZ *walking Stage Left as John watches* And that hooker looked just like that blonde tart you had the hots for last winter, remember? Your ideal woman — *Turns straight Front.* What was her name? Tech? Techka? *Liz turns.*

JOHN *coming behind Liz on Centre Stage* Thekla. But what is all this? We're on the Reserve now.

LIZ *confronting John, face to face* That's the point. The city is where you belong. It's the best place for you to accomplish what you feel you must do. To write.

JOHN *turning Front* But like Ida said, maybe I could be a writer here.

LIZ You better get wise to yourself. You won't be happy here and you know it.
Walks to Stage Right.
I know the first thing you're gonna do when you get back to the city. You're going to phone up 'Thekla'. Oh, I know you well, John.

JOHN *exasperated, moving from middle of dock, one step to Stage Right* There's more to life than women...

LIZ *walking toward John* Are you

sure? Seems that's the reason
you want to stay here.
Glares at John.
For a woman.
*Walks off as Josh and Paul
enter. John is silent, as if
discovering a truth, which may
well be, for the first time.*

JOSH *standing on Stage Left by
Dock* So, are you going to the
city? With Liz?

PAUL *standing on Stage Right by
Dock* Yes, and when he gets
there, he's going to leave her for
the German blonde. Right
John?

JOHN *going back upstage around to
Stage Right* Well, I'm thinking
of staying here.
*Paul and Josh follow John and
start to kid him.*

PAUL But if you do go, there's Thekla waiting...

JOSH And her being so religious and holy, you're gonna have to go to church a lot...

PAUL But with a good-looking woman like that, it'll be worth all those hours in church. Eh, John?

JOHN *going Front Stage Right* Cut it out, you guys.

JOSH Speaking of religious people, what ever happened to the holy roller that came to the Reserve and tried to save us last summer?

PAUL Old Moses, that Cree evangelist from Sandy Lake?

JOSH He used to be a drunken bum on the streets of Kenora before 'de Lord did save his soul'.

CHORUS *Paul and Josh* Amen.

JOSH   What's he doing now?

JOHN   Well, last I heard, he was holding revival meetings up at his home.

PAUL   One time this past spring, I was in Toronto and who do I see but Old Moses, trying to cross Yonge Street at 5 o'clock rush hour and this Jehovah's Witness comes up to him, *Pushes Josh down on knees.* grabs him by the scruff of the neck and gets ready to preach him the Gospel.

JOSH   *trying to get up*   A classical case of who will save who, huh?

PAUL   Poor Jehovah's Witness. He sure didn't know that lost-looking Cree was a devil-casting-out preacher, a brother of Jesus!

JOSH *trying to get up but Paul pushes him down again*   I'd bet my last dollar on Old Moses coming off best.

PAUL Old Moses may be lost in Toronto, but when it comes to the Lord and the Bible, look out, poor Jehovah's Witness!

JOSH Hear the word of the Lord!

PAUL *picking up a large frog*   Praise the Lord! Ribbit, Ribbit.

JOSH *being pursued by Paul to Back Stage Right*   Hey, get that frog out of here!

JOHN Throw that thing back into the water.
Comes up behind Paul and puts the frog into the water.

JOSH Remember Paul, when we were kids, we used to go around spearing frogs...

Gets on the Riser.
We'd take our jackknives and
sharpen our wooden stakes,
and yelling like the warriors we
were supposed to be –
Jumps off Riser.
we'd really do it to those
bullfrogs.

JOHN *standing at Centre Stage* I used
to spear bullfrogs myself.
Sometimes, I regret it but...

PAUL Well, those days're gone –
pretending to be warriors.
We're a different kind of
warrior now.

JOSH What do you mean?

PAUL Often I hear people cut me
down, just like we used to cut
down bullfrogs... But this time,
Gets on to Riser.

people are using words instead
of spears.

JOHN Word-spears, you mean.

PAUL And that really bugs me. Do
they think they're demi-gods or
something?

JOHN Demi-gods? People? What are
you talking about?

PAUL Well, like the way people act
without caring about others.
Like in Kenora, people there
don't care. Seems like they even
hate Indians. Like this old
Indian I saw slip at the stop
light the last time I was there.

JOSH What happened to the old guy?

PAUL *looking at Josh* I went over and
helped him up, and that old
Indian with his weather-lined
face and his baggy pants, he

could have been my
grandfather or yours. I guess
that's what really bothered me
in here.
Pats his heart.

JOSH That's really heavy stuff, Paul.
When were you there?

PAUL Last May, just before I came
back to the Reserve. But of that
old Indian, he slipped and fell
in the street and no one even
bothered to try to help. He
could have been run over by a
car. No, people just don't give a
damn about Indians.
Ida and Liz enter Stage Right.
Sound of light laughter.

JOSH Shhh! Here come the girls and
Ida has her camera.

PAUL She must want a picture of you

before you leave. I mean, you are leaving, when the plane comes, aren't you?

JOHN *moving towards Centre Stage* I don't know...

Ida takes John by the arm, shows him to the Small Riser, then walks to top of Dock.

IDA I want to take a picture of you. This one is for posterity.

CHORUS Come on John. Be serious.

A click indicates one picture is taken.

JOSH What was so funny, John?

JOHN Posterity.

PAUL What's so funny about that?

JOHN It reminded me of my Uncle Alex.

JOSH Your Uncle Alex must be around 70 years old.

JOHN *stepping down* 65 last October.

JOSH He sure gets around for a guy his age.

JOHN One morning while he was eating his breakfast of fried moosemeat, porridge, and Carnation milk, I grabbed my camera and took a photograph of him for posterity.
Turns to Centre Stage.
I sent the picture to the Wawatay News, and you know what?

LIZ He got his picture in the paper.

JOHN Right on the front page.

JOSH I saw that in the July issue!

PAUL Big time.

JOHN The funniest part was when I showed him his picture. He says,
Mimics his uncle's voice.
'Who's that?' 'Don't you

recognize that person?'
Again he mimics his uncle's voice.
'No, looks like some old woman.'
I said, 'That's you!' And you
know what he did?

CHORUS What did he do?

JOHN He threw back his head and
laughed at having made the
front page of the Wawatay
News…looking like some
refined old lady.

IDA That's part of the reason I like
your uncle. He's got a good
sense of humour. Not too many
people can laugh at themselves.
He is also a good storyteller.
What's that favourite of his,
something about a horse?

JOHN *mimicking his Uncle Alex's
voice* 'The White Horse will
gallop tonight.' Yes, he's fond of

telling that one. He would put his ear to the ground listening for the sound of horses' hooves. 'Back of the island, I saw the White Horse, his mane whipped like the moon against a black sky, and his eyes burned like embers of a dying forest fire, and fast he raced along the sandy shore, fast and faster still until his racing, thundering hooves carried him out of sight into...' I often wonder about such a White Horse.

Goes to Stage Right.

PAUL I used to think of a white horse, but with a cowboy like John Wayne riding it.

JOSH You got that from the movies

during our residential school days.

IDA When I was a little girl, my father would tell me stories and often about a White Horse.

LIZ You're saying it was true?

IDA So I was told.

JOHN Whether or not it was an actual fact, I remember him saying, that he'd seen the White Horse once...

Goes back to Centre Stage.

PAUL *going to Centre Stage* It is a good story and part of our heritage.

JOSH Maybe someday I'll paint that story.

JOHN *speaking sarcastically* Yes, for posterity.

LIZ *speaking to Paul* You're really

into our history, or should I use the word, 'heritage'?

PAUL Same thing. Proud to be Indian.

LIZ *going toward Paul* When did you start dressing up with your beads and feathers and old ragged jeans?

PAUL At least I don't dress like you or even John sometimes, straight out of Eaton's catalogue.

JOSH *speaking to Paul and getting up* Yes, when did you start going Native?

Ida also gets up beside Paul.

PAUL It began, in a way, with this necklace of turquoise and bear claws.

JOSH *grinning at Paul* Aw, those aren't real claws.

JOHN *speaking to Paul* Turquoise?

That looks like glass!

LIZ Who made the necklace?

PAUL The Mohawks of Akwesasne Reserve.

LIZ But we're Ojibway, Paul.

PAUL Ojibway, Mohawk, Cree, we're all Indians. And you guys better lay off. I'm damned proud to be Indian. See these moccasins –
Indicates his feet.
I got these at the Toronto Native Centre and I've worn them everywhere.

JOSH Even to bed?

PAUL *ignoring remark* I've worn these moccasins into the Department of Indian Affairs in Toronto, into and along the marble halls of the Royal

Ontario Museum. Yes, I showed
those people what a real Indian
is.

JOHN *stepping toward Paul* Paul,
being Indian isn't just the
clothes that you wear.

PAUL I'm proud to wear these clothes.
Points to John's city boots.
Look at you – even on the
Reserve, he wears his city
shoes.

LIZ What's with you?

PAUL You're one to talk – look at you.

LIZ When I'm on stage, I wear full
traditional Indian dress. Is that
old jean jacket, your A.I.M.
shirt, really Indian?

PAUL Maybe I'm not the old time
Indian.
*Does small dance in circle of
cast.*

And I don't perform a
traditional dance, but I'm a
modern Indian at least.
Strikes pose.
Listen! As Hollywood Indian, I
perform my Ojibway
raindance.

CHORUS Ojibway raindance?

PAUL *doing sign language for clouds*
and rain
When the weather charts tell
of rains to come
for
the Crest-gleaming teeth of the
  green-backed tourist
Goes to Dock and makes arm
movement.
I chant my song like a rolling
  stone
Takes a step and claps hands.
I clap my hands like a

back-firing engine
Takes a step and bounces.
I wriggle my hips like a belly
 dancer
Takes a step and smirks.
I flash my feet like a snake
 touching fool
Beat starts. Chorus begins
thigh-slapping.
As I dance – Wooooo –
Raindance!
Beat starts and Chorus comes
around dock.
Dancing 100-watt bulb
or
Prancing by moonlight
or
Lancing by firebug glow
Strikes pose.
I perform my raindance.

IDA Into the security of pocketbooks

JOSH Of the enriching Americans
Paul looks to audience in puzzlement of what's happening to his performance.

LIZ And that weather forecaster

CHORUS *crowding around Liz* Better be **damn** right!
All laugh. Go back to original positions .

IDA Where did you learn that?

PAUL In some book, Canadian Indian poetry, I think.
Pause.

JOSH *speaking to Liz* Why don't you show us what you do when you perform?

LIZ *getting up on Small Riser* Okay.
A mixture of Indian and known

*mime sign language is used to
enhance her performance.
Others seat themselves in
position.*
In days gone by,
the shadows of geese darkened
forests below
in forests where deer freely
roamed
Manitou walked with His
people then
His people, the Ojibway
riders in lavender dawns
masters of grey clouds,
the Ojibway
great, in days gone by

JOSH That's good.

PAUL Shhh!

LIZ In days gone by
the call of the loon

echoed freely on the rivers
and lakes
and the sound of the streams
was like laughter of children
playing
when Manitou talked with His
   people
His people, the Ojibway
riders in lavender dawns
masters of grey clouds
the Ojibway great
In days gone by
Others express appreciation.

LIZ *sitting* I also tell traditional
stories and legends since I
believe it is important to
present our past, the richness of
our culture and history.

PAUL And maybe I can't do that as
well as you but I want to do

something about the problems
of our people today and not just
talk about it.

LIZ I also tell of today. Like when
my father goes fishing in his
canoe.

JOSH You mean that old thing he's
re-canvassed at least ten times?

CHORUS *laughing* Shhh!
*Presentation of this poem is less
formal.*

LIZ Morning comes often like a
glass mirror
on the summer waters of
Kejick Bay.
In Kejick Bay, the Ojibway
have lived
hundreds of lives as fishermen
And my father, he pushes out
his canoe

to check his gill nets. He licks
    his lips,
thinking of yellow pickerel
    sizzling
in his black frying pan.
Four hundred feet off shore,
    loons ride low
in the water.
They do not fly away when
    my father,
Ojibway fisherman paddles
    slowly by.
And later, my father
    smiles at the pickerel
he trails over the side
    of his canoe,
flicks the ash of his pipe onto
    the scales of mud suckers.
He watches the terns flitting
    over the glass-like surface

of Kejick Bay,
as again, he picks up his
    paddle and
with no need for haste, or to
    hurry,
he paddles home to breakfast,
as bulrushes on the shoreline
bend in the first wind touches
on summer water morning of
    Kejick Bay,
just like in history over
    hundreds
of years of the Ojibway.
Chorus express appreciation.
Clap hands, etc.

PAUL   Why don't you ever write like
       that, John?

JOHN   I don't know. I guess, I …

LIZ   Sometimes you bug me with
      that humility or lack of
      confidence, whatever it is. He

wrote that for me last winter.
When I needed new material, I
asked him for some, that was
just a sample of it.

PAUL Did you ever think of writing
about the social problems of our
people?

JOHN I think I know what you mean.
But if you mean, bitter and
angry stuff, No. I wrote a poem
about Gerald Bannatyne from
Ear Falls. I called it 'Folk Hero'.

PAUL Hah! Him a Folk Hero? Hah!

JOHN *getting up* He is to me.

PAUL Did you ever get that poem or
whatever it was, published
anywhere besides our own
newspaper?

JOHN *walking around between Paul
and Liz* Well, the poem made it
to the Ear Falls Observer.

PAUL Small town newspaper!

IDA Say the poem. I remember
reading it, it's nothing to be
ashamed of.
Steps into place.

JOHN Well, here goes:
*John's voice and movements
betray his nervousness. Josh
moves up beside Ida.*
Gerald Bannatyne recounts the
   experiences
of 60 years up and down
the shores of Lac Seul.
Other men have their Lake
   Superior
and Leif the Lucky had his
   ocean.
Gerald Bannatyne is the local
   passage to
history and nostalgia.

Even people in Ear Falls need a
    folk hero
Gerald Bannatyne didn't waste
    his lungs
building a dream castle for a
woman who didn't want him
And to this day, Gerald
    Bannatyne
breathes out his memories
from his log cabin
for the Ear Falls Observer
stories of integrity
and lies
up and down the shores
of Lac Seul.
Chorus claps, cheers, etc.
JOHN *standing Front Centre*
    Stage That wasn't so hard.
PAUL *standing Centre Stage* I'm
    sorry I didn't read that

newspaper but, some of that other stuff he had published in our Wawatay News was pretty mushy.

Everyone except John freezes.

TRANSITION TO INTROSPECT

JOHN *speaking to Paul* Mushy?
Faces Stage Left
Maybe it was mushy. Inconsistent. But what really bothers me is that I'm not committed to anything. Am I a literary critic? Am I qualified to judge my own work?
Others come alive.

TRANSITION TO REALITY

PAUL *turning to John* I don't think

your published work has been
all that helpful.

JOHN *turning to Paul* As I recall, you
admitted that you didn't read
that much.

PAUL *moving forward toward
John* What I'm saying is that
you can use your time better by
writing articles about the
Ojibway people who are being
exploited.

JOHN *going to left corner of Riser* If
you're so concerned, why don't
you get off your ass and do
something instead of
criticizing.

PAUL *standing Centre Stage and
speaking to Cast* I am, that's
why I'm leaving when the
plane comes in.
Speaks to John.

Are you going to be able to make up your mind on what to do by then?

JOHN *stepping up front* Well, I'm...

PAUL *speaking to John* You don't know if you're coming or going. *Looks at Cast and points at John.*

The uncommitted writer. As for me, I'm going up to Grassy Narrows.

JOSH Isn't that the Reserve where people have to eat contaminated fish?

PAUL *speaking to Cast* Yes. And do you know that pulp and paper mill in Dryden has polluted the English/Wabicoon River system and now the Indians of that area who depend on fishing for a living are out of

work. And if they eat the fish,
they'll get mercury in their
blood?

JOHN I read that in the paper.

PAUL *speaking to John* You read it
and you're not concerned?

JOHN Yes, I am. But what can I do?

PAUL *speaking to John* You could
write about it from the Native
perspective, for Christ's sake!
Speaks to Cast.
Now the poor Natives of Grassy
Narrows have that sickness,
Minamata Disease, and all
because of the Whiteman's
greed.

JOHN Isn't our government doing
something about it?

PAUL Not really. All they do is ask
the Indians
Speaks to Ida, falsetto voice

'Please don't eat the fishes!'
And they try to ease their
conscience by importing fresh
fish to feed those poor sick
people.

JOHN Which is just another form of
welfare.

PAUL John, you do understand! Like,
they don't stop Americans from
fishing because Americans
bring in lots of money. But do
you know what the government
does?

JOHN *nodding* What? Tell me.
Sits on Large Riser.

PAUL They are trying to stop those
Indians from fishing and
fishing is what the people have
done for centuries. And then
tried to buy off the people by

proposing to build a national park there.

JOHN But not all white people treat Indians badly.

PAUL Well, you can say that since you only hang around the artist crowd when you do go off the Reserve.

JOHN *getting up* Paul, you're really uptight today. Relax. Everyone is entitled to their own opinion.

PAUL Yeah! You're right. But I'm not angry at you or anyone else here. It's just...remembering that gets me sore.
Gives John the A.I.M. *handshake (clasping thumbs).* Look, it's the white people who brought alcohol to the Indian and now mercury on top of the

alcohol problem is just too
much.
Goes up front.
That's why I'm going to Grassy
Narrows.

JOHN And if you let that bitterness
stay with you, you'll end up
becoming an active member of
the American Indian
Movement, a radical that will
be prosecuted and harrassed by
police.

PAUL Maybe so, but if I hear any
more songs like
Speaks in monotone.
one little, two little, three little
Indians
Resumes normal voice.
I'm going to get real angry. God,
that song bugs me.

JOHN *getting up* Our people are starting to become politically involved; think of my friend Donnie.

PAUL Donnie! Him? some friend! Why, I remember the last time we saw him. He didn't help us. No, he didn't help us at all.

JOHN What are you talking about?

PAUL Here, let me show you. Josh – Filing Clerk; Liz – Secretary; Ida – Receptionist; John, you play yourself coming down the marble hallway to the door. I'll be Donnie standing behind his desk.

TRANSITION TO INTROSPECT

John knocks on door marked

*'Donald J. Brown'. This scene is
acted in caricature except for
John.*

RECEPTIONIST *opening door* Come in, can I
help you?

JOHN Tell Donnie, John the writer, is
here to see him.

RECEPTIONIST Mr. Brown? I'll have to ask his
secretary if he's busy.

JOHN Receptionist? Red carpet?
Panelled walls? Secretary?
*Receptionist, Secretary, and Mr.
D. Brown speak in undertones.*

RECEPTIONIST A John, the writer, is here to
see Mr.Brown.

SECRETARY Mr. Brown, there's a John, the
writer here to see you.

MR. D. BROWN Send three copies of these over
to the Minister's office right
away.

Paul's right hand is under his T shirt to caricature a fat bureaucrat.
Speaks to John. Secretary and receptionist freeze.
Yes, can I help you?
John leaves the room and slams the door.

TRANSITION TO REALITY

JOHN Just another goddamn bureaucrat!

PAUL And if you're not careful, you'll leave the Reserve and be just like that so-called friend of yours, just another goddamn bureaucrat. Get what I mean?

JOHN Sure I understand, Paul. I'm not stupid.

PAUL Yeah. He's an apple Indian and you're becoming one. Apple as in red on the outside and white on the inside.
Paul and John move into Centre Stage for confrontation.

JOHN *speaking coldly* Is that so?
Ida and Liz come to break tension. Josh watches over Liz's shoulder.

PAUL Apple. John the apple. The uncommitted writer.

IDA and LIZ Come on, you guys!

IDA Stop it. Paul, what is this? Intertribal warfare? We're supposed to be friends.
Cast freezes.

TRANSITION TO INTROSPECT

JOHN Intertribal warfare?

Cast walks off. Ida stops in tears as John turns to the audience.

TRANSITION TO REALITY

IDA *coming Front* I see you've decided to leave... What did Liz say to make you change your mind?

JOHN It wasn't anything she said...

IDA Sure. You seemed to change after you talked to her.

JOHN I'm my own man. My dad always says I should make up my own mind. Whenever I left before he shook my hand and said, 'until the next time'.

IDA But I know it hurts him.

JOHN *speaking half seriously, half jokingly* You know, Indians don't cry.

IDA That's not true. Last winter when you left after Christmas I saw tears in your father's eyes, and as the plane grew smaller, stillness would fill the air, then we would all go home and not a word could be heard because of heartaches.

JOHN Don't they know? I'll always come back, even if it's just for a visit.

IDA Why did you stay?

JOHN *going to Dock and sitting* An Ojibway legend came true for me. Last June, shortly after I came back from Toronto. It was one hot, T-shirt-clinging morning. I couldn't sleep, mosquitoes were driving me crazy. They must have gotten past the screens my father had set up. And Mom, she was angry because of the sickness in her lungs. She was swirling around the inside of our cabin, like a dragon fly slashing at the insects. I was afraid of her anger. It was then I heard the trembling and soft calls of the Death Bird. I didn't tell Dad, and now it's too late. My mother rode off with the Death Bird three weeks ago. Damned Death Bird! Stupid legend!

IDA   Now I understand why you had to stay.

JOHN   I should know that death is no stranger. And you, I remember how your mom stood silent by the grave of her husband.

IDA She was proud of my father for he gave us life, food and shelter. It is part of our Ojibway people.

JOHN Not too many people can leave such a legacy.

IDA I remember how happy my parents were. Every morning my father would get up and start a fire in the wood stove. Then he would make a pot of fresh Red Rose tea 'cause that's what my mother liked first thing in the morning.

JOHN My dad still does...

IDA And I remember when we were camping one summer. I saw them going out with the mosquito tent and down to a quiet stream and I remember

my parents making love and
my mother would cry. It was so
beautiful. At the same time I
would hear the wind blowing
through the trees.
Chorus members roll onto the
stage to become elements.
Sound of the wind.
The smell of pine filled the air.
All working like man and
Nature, all in harmony as it
should be. We could be like
that. Look at the beauty of
Nature and those docks. Aren't
they beautiful?
Chorus members move up on
John and Ida.
Sound of birds.

JOHN They are all gathering together
to fly south, just like the geese

will in the near future. Listen
to them fly.

*Chorus members Paul and Liz
join arms together to become
twin engine plane.*

*Sound of an airplane by Paul,
Liz and Josh. Low volume but
rising.*

IDA It's the airplane, John! There it
is!

JOHN I got to go.

IDA See how noisy it is. It'll be just
like that in the city.

JOHN I have to leave. I must try...

IDA Please stay with us. I need you.

JOHN I've got to prove myself out in
the city...

*Airplane sound growing louder
and louder.*

IDA Your father needs you.

JOHN   My father understands.
*Plane comes in, taxis to dock.
John shakes Josh's hand. He
hugs Ida, and climbs aboard
the plane. John then becomes
the plane's pilot.*
I am my own man. I'm in
control of my own destiny.
*Ida and Josh wave goodbye
then walk away. Plane takes off.
Becomes train. Train wheels
make sound of 'John, John,
John'. John becomes train
engine followed by Liz and
Paul. Ida and Josh at a railway
station.*

CONDUCTOR: JOSH
All aboard! Sioux Lookout, city
and civilization. One thousand
miles.

Ida as a passenger climbs on board. Train leaves. Conductor starts the John sounds to imitate sound of a train engine starting up.John sounds are heard throughout low but steady.

VOICE 1: LIZ Boy!

John...

VOICE 2: PAUL Dreams!

John...

VOICE 3: JOSH Wheels!

John...

VOICE 4: IDA Train!

John...

CONDUCTOR: JOSH

Two hundred miles to Sault Ste. Marie!

John...

Pause.

Sault Ste. Marie!

John...

VOICE 1: LIZ Running!
Wheels!
Thundering!
Factories!
Sky-scrapers!

CONDUCTOR: JOSH
Toronto Union Station!

JOHN My mind with its light
flashing, the steel wheel
speeding charges
in
my always dreamer soul...
*Train slows to stop at
dock-platform. John is jostled,
squeezed by two male and two
female riders. All struggle to get
on platform. John squeezes
away to the front (edge of
platform). John freezes
momentarily. The two male and*

73

female riders also freeze,
jostling. Subway sounds of
starting up—Chorus. Train
starts. Paul steps front—
momentary glance to John.

PAUL I don't know this October
      Stranger,
      each dawn groping for an alarm
      clock,
      selecting a blue polyester suit
      that used to belong to an Indian
      from the backforests of
      northwestern Ontario.
      Sounds of the train by Chorus.
      Subway train stopping. Paul
      steps back on. Train goes. Josh
      steps front. Momentary glance
      to John.

JOSH This autumn stranger washes a
      once familiar face,

runs windburnt fingers over a
cowlick topped head of black
   hair,
the exact image of a man I
swear
I once knew.
*Subway train stops. (Sound effect
— Chorus)*

LIZ *going Front — Momentary
   glance*
This October Stranger adjusts
   his blue tie,
flips through documents before
   sliding
them into a $40-briefcase
and then rides off on a rocking
   subway train
to his second-storey office
on Eglinton Avenue East in
   Toronto.

Stops. (Sound effects – Chorus).

JOHN *going Front, looking straight
ahead* I don't know this
autumn stranger
that writes his stories
and poems
as if Chaucer himself was
  kicking
him along, never letting him
  rest,
this Indian dedicated to
  becoming published.
*Subway train stops. (Sound
effects – Chorus).*

IDA *going Front, looking towards
John* I don't know this
October Stranger
that left a love of three years
behind without a kiss;
*Train keeps going. Train slows
down, then goes.*

JOHN *looking to the audience* This
autumn stranger that knew
his 64-year-old father is left
all alone in a log cabin
on the Lac Seul Indian Reserve
and yet

CHORUS: IDA, JOSH, LIZ, AND PAUL
*looking towards John, turning
heads front* Migrated south.

JOHN *to audience* I don't know this
October Stranger.
*Sound of train stopping by
Chorus. Doors opened by Liz
and Paul — exit first followed by
Ida, Josh and John. State of
exasperation, silent meaning.
John is silent. Liz and Paul
close the door and all leave the
stage. John is swallowed up by
the crowd made up of the
Chorus members.*

77